This is the true story of Little Larry,
an orphan chimpanzee who was once afraid
to climb trees, but learned to be brave.

NATIONAL
GEOGRAPHIC
KiDS

Little Larry
Goes to School

The True Story of a Timid Chimpanzee
Who Learned to Reach New Heights

Gerry Ellis
With **Mary Rand Hess**

NATIONAL GEOGRAPHIC
WASHINGTON, D.C.

On a misty African morning, a baby chimpanzee was born. It was the rainy season at the sanctuary, and heavy showers loomed. Just days later, there was an accident that left the newborn badly hurt. A human caregiver had to take the orphan chimp and nurse him back to health. He named him Little Larry.

For months, the caregiver fed and cuddled Little Larry and cleaned up after him. He even slept with the chimp at night to keep him safe.

Little Larry had a lot to learn to get along with other chimpanzees. The caregiver taught Little Larry how to groom himself by using his fingers to brush through hair. Grooming is important for Little Larry to stay clean, and also because chimps groom each other to show they want to be friends.

The caregiver hooted, screeched, and stomped with Little Larry to teach him how chimps talk to each other. Little Larry also climbed up on his caregiver's back to practice using his hands to pull his way up. He needed this skill to climb forest trees one day.

When Little Larry was eight months old, he was ready for his first playdate with another young chimp, named Daphne. They toddled around, groomed each other, and explored their cozy enclosure. But this was not enough to prepare Little Larry for life in the big sanctuary.

Daphne (left) and Little Larry

Little Larry (right) and one of his classmates

When he turned a year old, it was time for Little Larry to meet other orphan chimps at the forest school. There, they could practice climbing cacao trees. Knowing how to climb trees was important, so the chimps could play and search for food. They needed to learn how to find a quiet branch when there was a squabble with another chimp, or how to escape from dangers on the ground, like snakes.

Each morning, Little Larry held hands with his chimp classmates—Daphne, Paula, Lil Jenny, and Lomié—and walked to school.

Sometimes, Little Larry became excited and ran ahead of everyone. But each time, his caregiver made a loud *ooh ooh* sound and called him back to the group.

Lil Jenny (left) and Lomié

Paula and Daphne climb in the trees.

When they reached the forest school, Little Larry knuckle-walked into the grove. The trees shook in the wind. Daphne, Paula, Lil Jenny, and Lomié were ready to practice jumping and climbing. They grabbed on to branches, bounced on their feet, and leaped from limb to limb. But not Little Larry. He stayed on the ground. He wasn't ready to be up high, swinging from the trees.

While the others took off, Little Larry
found a log to sit on. He seemed scared.

After sitting and watching the other chimps, Little Larry searched for sticks, roots, and cacao leaves. He met a giant millipede and poked it with his fingers, as if determined to make a new friend. It seemed like he almost forgot about climbing and his friends high above him.

At mealtime, everyone came out of the trees and back to the ground. A caregiver arrived with papayas, avocados, mangoes, and other fruits. Little Larry sucked on juicy watermelon from his caregiver's hand. When they finished eating, the chimps all cuddled together for a peaceful afternoon rest.

Lil Jenny and Lomié

After naptime, the chimps mostly stayed on
the ground. They wrestled and played silly
games, like investigating each other's long
pink tongues. Now and again, Daphne would go
out of her way to tease Little Larry. She snatched
a yummy piece of mango from his grasp.

Daphne zipped up a vine and escaped with the stolen goody, tempting Little Larry to chase her up the tree. Little Larry balanced on his knuckles and stomped back and forth to let everyone know that he was not happy.

But he stayed firmly on the ground.

After weeks of being teased and watching the other chimps climb high above him, Little Larry grabbed a vine. It was only inches off the ground. He tried to swing, but fell. Then he grabbed hold again. This time he spun, twisted, and turned. He even hung upside down on a low-hanging limb. It wasn't *really* climbing, but it was a start.

His caregiver tried to get Little Larry to climb higher, onto the branches of a nearby tree. Little Larry crawled up the trunk. But then he looked down. It must have been frightening to be up so high, because Little Larry scurried back down to the ground. Up a little bit, then back down he climbed. This went on for weeks.

But with each and every try, Little Larry became more confident. He swung his arms and legs to get momentum. He used his fingers and toes to grasp the branches. Higher and higher he moved up the cacao tree. After months of practicing, Little Larry finally reached the top and proudly looked out over his world.

Little Larry graduated from the forest school and joined the older chimps in the big sanctuary. This map shows Little Larry's home and other places chimpanzees live in Africa.

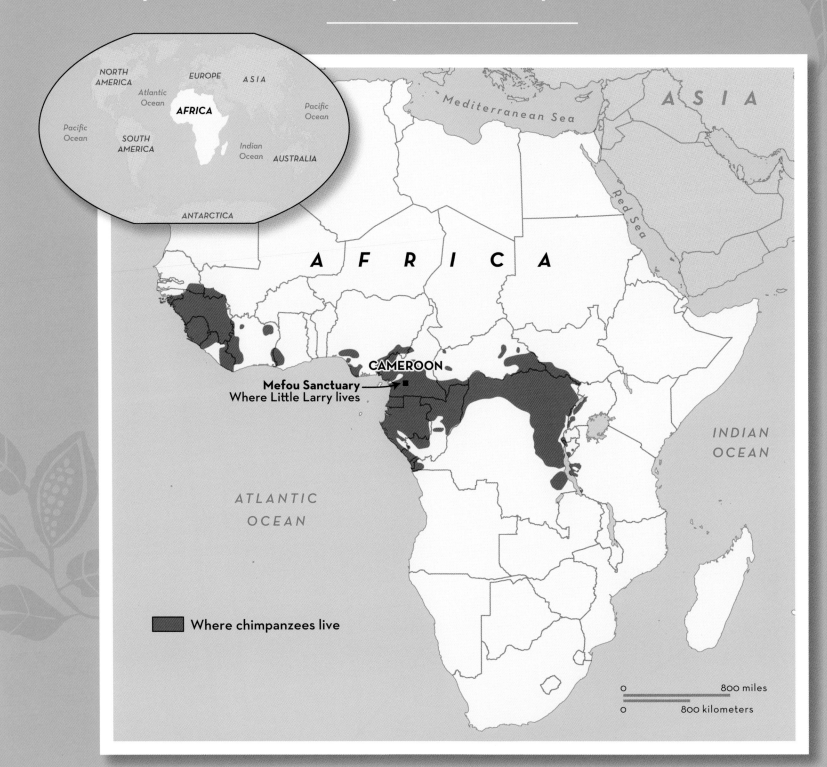

NORTH AMERICA

EUROPE

ASIA

Atlantic Ocean

AFRICA

Pacific Ocean

Pacific Ocean

SOUTH AMERICA

Indian Ocean

AUSTRALIA

ANTARCTICA

Mediterranean Sea

ASIA

Red Sea

AFRICA

CAMEROON

Mefou Sanctuary
Where Little Larry lives

INDIAN OCEAN

ATLANTIC OCEAN

Where chimpanzees live

0   800 miles

0   800 kilometers

Speak like Little Larry

Little Larry's hoots, barks, squeaks, and grunts add up to many things he wants other chimps and his human caretakers to know. Humans understand more than 30 different vocal calls chimpanzees make.

Try making these three chimp sounds and see if you can speak like Little Larry.

THE FOOD GRUNT

HOW TO DO IT:
Make two *eeh* noises that sound like a squeaky burst coming from your throat. Then make two *ah* sounds.

WHAT IT MEANS:
When Little Larry is excited to eat something he really loves, like mango, he uses this sound. He often has his hands out with his palms up, or is shaking an open hand, as if he is saying, "Please! I really want some."

THE PLAY FACE

HOW TO DO IT:
Open your mouth in a wide smile, then curl your upper and lower lips over your teeth. Breathe in and out very fast as you giggle.

WHAT IT MEANS:
Chimps love to laugh. If Little Larry is tickled in the armpits or around his neck, he will start giggling and make the play face to show he's having fun.

THE PANT-HOOT

HOW TO DO IT:
Put your lips together and push them forward like you are going to kiss something. Make a quiet *hoo* sound, then get louder with longer *hoos*. Finish with a small yell.

WHAT IT MEANS:
The pant-hoot is one of the most common sounds Little Larry will make in his whole life. It can be a greeting, a way to show he's excited about food, or a chance to say, "Hey, I'm here, what are you guys doing?"

Want to learn more about chimpanzees?

ABOUT APE ACTION AFRICA

Ape Action Africa is a nonprofit organization that rescues orphan chimps, gorillas, and monkeys in Cameroon. The orphans are cared for at Mefou Sanctuary, where they can grow healthy and strong and live together in large areas of forest. Mefou Sanctuary is also a place where visitors can learn why these animals are endangered and how people can protect them from extinction.

WEBSITES

Ape Action Africa: See how you can help endangered chimpanzees and other apes.
apeactionafrica.org

National Geographic Kids: Explore facts, photos, and range maps for kids, parents, and educators.
natgeokids.com/animals/chimpanzee

Apes Like Us: Watch Gerry Ellis's fun, humorous, and educational videos on chimpanzees and other apes.
youtube.com/apeslikeus

Pan African Sanctuary Alliance (PASA): Learn more about primates and check out other wildlife sanctuaries in Africa.
pasaprimates.org

BOOKS

Chimpanzee Children of Gombe by Jane Goodall, with photographs by Michael Neugebauer

Little Chimp (Mini Look at Me Books) by Laura Rigo

My Life With the Chimpanzees by Jane Goodall

The Watcher: Jane Goodall's Life With the Chimps by Jeanette Winter

Facts about chimpanzees

- Chimps are not monkeys. They are in the ape family. One way you can tell the difference is that monkeys have tails and apes do not.

- Chimps use tools like sticks to find insects and stones to crack open nuts.

- Chimps use a complex language of sounds and gestures to communicate with each other.

- A close-knit community of chimpanzees is called a troop.

- Chimps can live between 40 and 50 years in the wild and up to 60 years in captivity.

- These apes are endangered because most of their habitats are being destroyed. They are also at risk of going extinct because of the pet trade and animal poaching. This means there are not many chimps left in the wild or in our world's sanctuaries.

A note from the photographer

Little Larry pulls on the elastic strap on the back of photographer Gerry Ellis's glasses. Little Larry was obsessed with stealing Ellis's glasses, and the strap was supposed to prevent that from happening.

When my water taxi (an overcrowded wooden boat) pulled up on the beach 30 years ago at Gombe Stream, Tanzania, the research site of famed primatologist Jane Goodall, I didn't know that my life would forever after include chimpanzees. Big and hairy, small and cute, the chimps were wild—pant-hooting and eating figs 66 feet (20 m) above the forest floor (although habituated a bit by Dr. Goodall). That is how, for many years, I saw and thought of chimps—wild.

In 1993 that belief changed. While I was filming mountain gorillas in Rwanda, two baby chimps were confiscated from poachers at the border of Rwanda and the Democratic Republic of the Congo. Veterinarians held them in a cage near Virunga National Park headquarters and worked to find a suitable future home for them. I expected to film them and go, but instead my heart was torn. I sat crying outside their cage, as these two little babies reached through the bars, begging for contact. Chimps are apes, like us, and need love, contact, and care. For the first time, I witnessed the horrific tragedy of poaching and the illegal ape trade that has now devastated wild great ape populations across equatorial Africa (and orangutan populations on the Asian islands of Borneo and Sumatra).

The past quarter century has not been kind to apes or their habitat. Wild ape populations that once numbered more than one million are now below 200,000 and are still shrinking as you read this. Why do I film great apes? I'm desperate to tell the world what is happening to our closest cousins. My great fear is one day being asked by a child, "Tell me what a chimp or gorilla was."

Little Larry is a wonderful, brilliant little chimpanzee. I have rarely had as much fun filming as I did with him, Daphne, Lomié, Paula, and Lil Jenny. Every day was a joyride of childhood adventures, exploration, and chaos. But as wonderful as the amazing people of Ape Action Africa and their work are, these are chimps that are not, and never will be, wild again.

Sanctuaries have become the lifeboats to a sinking wild ark.

When I first arrived at Ape Action Africa's Mefou Sanctuary, I met more than a dozen orphan chimps all under the age of six. As I began filming Little Larry and his forest school classmates, more orphans arrived, and they continue to arrive. Just at Mefou alone, a baby orphan chimp or western lowland gorilla arrives on average every three months. And the orphans who arrive are the lucky ones. They have now found sanctuary, peace, and care thanks to Ape Action Africa.

The illegal ape trade and poaching that I witnessed 25 years ago continue to this day, as does great ape habitat destruction. We must keep trying to end these threats to wild great apes, no matter how small the action. But it is also so important to help those dedicated, courageous, and compassionate people who are working in wildlife sanctuaries, trying to make the lives of orphan great apes valuable.

—Gerry Ellis

Credits

**This is for Rachel Hogan, whose passion, dedication, and devotion to apes
and all life hooked me the day I met her. Neither primatologist, conservationist,
nor politician, she works from the heart. And it's to her heart this book is dedicated.
—Gerry Ellis**

For Bella, keep climbing —M.R.H.

Text and Photographs Copyright © 2019 Gerry Ellis

Compilation Copyright © 2019 National Geographic Partners, LLC

Published by National Geographic Partners, LLC. All rights reserved. Reproduction of the whole or any part of the contents without written permission from the publisher is prohibited.

Since 1888, the National Geographic Society has funded more than 12,000 research, exploration, and preservation projects around the world. The Society receives funds from National Geographic Partners, LLC, funded in part by your purchase. A portion of the proceeds from this book supports this vital work. To learn more, visit natgeo.com/info.

NATIONAL GEOGRAPHIC and Yellow Border Design are trademarks of the National Geographic Society, used under license.

For more information, visit nationalgeographic.com, call 1-800-647-5463, or write to the following address:

National Geographic Partners
1145 17th Street N.W.
Washington, D.C. 20036-4688 U.S.A.

Visit us online at nationalgeographic.com/books

For librarians and teachers: ngchildrensbooks.org

More for kids from National Geographic: natgeokids.com

National Geographic Kids magazine inspires children to explore their world with fun yet educational articles on animals, science, nature, and more. Using fresh storytelling and amazing photography, *Nat Geo Kids* shows kids ages 6 to 14 the fascinating truth about the world—and why they should care. kids.nationalgeographic.com/subscribe

For information about special discounts for bulk purchases, please contact National Geographic Books Special Sales: specialsales@natgeo.com

For rights or permissions inquiries, please contact National Geographic Books Subsidiary Rights: bookrights@natgeo.com

The publisher would like to thank everyone who worked to make this book come together: Angela Modany, associate editor; Shannon Hibberd, senior photo editor; Mike McNey, map production; Molly Reid, production editor; and Anne LeongSon and Gus Tello, design production assistants.

Designed by Sanjida Rashid

National Geographic supports K–12 educators with ELA Common Core Resources. Visit natgeoed.org/commoncore for more information.

All other photos Copyright © Gerry Ellis, unless noted here. Photos below: cacao pods, Norman Chan/Shutterstock; mask, De Agostini/G. Dagli Orti/Getty Images.

Hardcover ISBN: 978-1-4263-3316-3
Reinforced library binding ISBN: 978-1-4263- 3317-0

Printed in China
18/PPS/1

A NOTE ON THE DESIGN

Little Larry lives in Cameroon, a country of verdant forests and diverse cultures. The visual themes used throughout the design of this book are inspired by the flora and artwork of Little Larry's home country. For instance, the cacao pods and lush vines found in the rain forests Larry and his friends roam adorn the page backgrounds. The color palette and triangle border pattern were chosen to reflect colors and patterns that are heavily featured in the artwork and textiles of various ethnic groups throughout Cameroon.

Left: Cacao tree pods (*Theobroma cacao*)

Right: A red, white, and black two-faced mask from Cameroon